The Asian Theatre School and Red Ladder
Theatre Company proudly presents

silent cry

Created by the **Asian Theatre School**

Written by **Madani Younis**

First performance of this production 15 September 2004

Cast 2004

Nasreen Hussain	**Safia Ahmed**
Sanjiv Hayre	**Bashir Ahmed**
Kashif Khan	**Nadeem Ahmed**
Bhavini Raval	**Noreen Ahmed**
Dharmesh Patel	**Shahid Khan**
Amelia Saberwal	**Nina Desai**
Mohammed Irfan	**PC1**
Ivan Stott	**PC2**

Written by	Madani Younis
Directors	Madani Younis & Sarah Brigham
Assistant Director	Wakas Zamurad
Dramaturgy by	Seamus Finnegan
Set Designer	Leslie Travers
Composer	Ivan Stott
Additional Vocals	Nusrat Bhatti
Lighting Design	Jeremy Nicholls
Visuals Director	Jeremy Nicholls
Set Build	Marcus Rapley – MJR Theatre Services
Stage Manager	Martin Toomer
Graphics Designer	Barry Darnell
Cover Photography	Duncan Grant

Red Ladder Management Team

Wendy Harris	Artistic Director
Janis Smyth	Financial Administrator
Deborah Palmer	Interim Company Administrator
Stefanie Gascoigne	Touring & Development Manager
Madani Younis	Asian Theatre School Director
Emma Melling	Assistant Administrator
Wakas Zamurad	Administrative Assistant

Cast 2003

Lubna Shuja	**Safia Ahmed**
Rafique Butt	**Bashir Ahmed**
Kashif Khan	**Nadeem Ahmed**
Lena Kaur	**Noreen Ahmed**
Asif Khan	**Shahid Khan**
Shaida Choudhury	**Nina Desai**
Madani Younis	**PC1**
Zahir Daji	**PC2**

Written by	Madani Younis
Directors	Madani Younis & Sarah Brigham
Assistant Director	Wakas Zamurad
Dramaturgy by	Andrea Earl
Set Designer	Leslie Travers
Choreography	Jason James
Composer	Ivan Stott
Additional Vocals	Nusrat Bhatti
Lighting Design	Marcus Rapley
Set Build	MJR Theatre Services
Stage Manager	Marcus Rapley / Chris Selkirk
Press Officer	Lisa Baxter

Thank you to:

The families of all those who have lost loved ones in Police custody for allowing us the opportunity to hear your stories. Thank you to the families of Christopher Alder, Harry Stanley, and the work of Terry Stewart.

Arts Council of Yorkshire & England for your continuing belief and support of our work. University of Bradford Theatre in the Mill, Bradford Theatres & Twisting Yarn, and the West Yorkshire Playhouse, Leeds for the opportunity to create and share our work with you.

Ruth Price, Karen Morris, Yvonne Terry, Lisa Baxter, Jatinder Verma, Manjinder Virk, Neil Biswas, Chris Johnstone, Janet Steel, our brothers and sisters from the Studio Theatre Damascus, Syria, and all those that have given so much to the success of this project.

Finally, thank you to every single actor that has passed through the doors of the Asian Theatre School, you have helped to invest and nurture the growth of this project beyond our wildest dreams. Without you none of this would ever have been possible. It has been a privilege to have worked with you all.

Biographies

Sanjiv Hayre Bashir Ahmed

Sanjiv trained at Central and the NWS Theatre School. He was the lead singer/guitarist in the band 'Damn Noisy Asians' (DNA). Recent stage work: The Doctor in Paul Burtill's *The Lodger* (Pentameters) and Haroon Amir in *Buddha of Suburbia*. Feature film credits include Abdul Sulaman in Prodigal Productions' *The Plague* and most recently former porn star Silas Daly in the comedy *Crooked Features* by Harp 28.

Nasreen Hussain Safia Ahmed

Nasreen trained at Bretton Hall University College of Leeds. Theatre credits include Indra's Daughter in *The Dream Play* (Powerhouse 1 Theatre), Scheherazade in *Harem* (2000 Edinburgh Fringe Festival); Miss Julie in *Miss Julie* (White Bear). Television credits include *Merseybeat*, *Casualty*, *Doctors*, *Outside the Rules*, *Blue Peter*, *Perfect*, *Crossroads*, *Barbara* III, *Murder Squad*. Radio Credits include Double Income No Kids Yet (BBC Radio 4).

Kashif Khan Nadeem Ahmed

Kashif has trained with the Asian Theatre School for three years. During his time there he has performed in Productions such as *Streets of Rage* (West Yorkshire Playhouse, Leeds), *Freeworld* (Contact Theatre, Manchester), and both the regional and national tour of *Silent Cry*.

Bhavini Raval Noreen Ahmed

Bhavini trained at Bretton Hall. Since graduating she has worked as an actor and a director. In collaboration with the British Council, Live Theatre UK, and Five Arts Centre, Kuala Lumpar, she was co-founder of ADA APA Touring Theatre Company in Malaysia. Her professional credits include *Silent Cry*, *Street Voices*, *Carnival Messiah* (West Yorkshire Playhouse). Her film credits include *Martha meet Frank Daniel and Lawrence*. Bhavini has also presented for Sabrang Radio. Television credits include *A Touch of Frost*, *Steel*, *River Blues*, *Blue Murder* and *Bodies*. Bhavini was the co-director of the Asian theatre School production *Freeworld* (Contact Theatre, Manchester).

Dharmesh Patel Shahid Khan

Dharmesh graduated from Liverpool John Moores University with a BA Hons degree in Drama. He then studied physical theatre at Hope Street Ltd. His theatre credits include: Dini in *Bollywood Jane* at Leicester Haymarket Theatre; Benjamin in *Animal Farm* for Angels Theatre Company (Italian Tour); The Charity Commissioner in *The Government Inspector*, *Beauty And The Beast*, *No Fear*, all at the Unity Theatre for Hope Street Ltd.; Harry in *Dirk And Harry*, Micky in *Mojo*, Jason in *Boxing*, Ensemble in *Pericles*, all for Liverpool John Moores University. His television credits include: Imran in *England Expects* for the BBC. On radio, Dharmesh plays the leading character of Arun Chauhan in *Silver Street* for the BBC Asian Network. Dharmesh has recorded various voiceovers for Talen Computers.

Amelia Saberwal Nina Desai

Amelia studied at Webber Douglas. She is very proud to say that *Silent Cry* is her first professional job since graduating a couple of months ago. Theatre Credits include *Present Laughter* (Drayton Arms), *Pride and Prejudice* (Tour), *The School for Scandal* and *The Laramie Project* (Chanticleer Theatre).

Martin Toomer Stage Manager

Martin has spent the last eighteen years in the business and has worked all over the world. He started out as stage crew for such names as *Elton john, Status Quo,* and other world-renowned names. Martin then moved onto work as stage manager, his credits include *Elton John* (Wembley), *Sting* (UK Dates), *Status Quo* (UK Tour 2001), and *Flying Music's Production of Hollywood and Broadway* (UK Tour), *Meredith Productions, Jack and the Bean Stalk* (Gracie Fields, Rochdale), also a world tour with *Gabrielle* on her *Rise* World Tour. Since this time Martin has worked at many of the UK's top festivals, *Glastonbury, Cambridge, Sidmouth, Stroud,* to name a few. In the last few years Martin has taken on a new challenge of Tour Management, and was Tour Manager for *Phoenix Productions UK Tours of Time Warp, Legends of Swing and Legends of Country, Phantom and the Opera,* and the early part of 2004 with the *Tony Hadley, Peter Cox and Go West UK Tour,* and just before joining Red Ladder Theatre Company, a UK tour with *Keppa Junkera* from Spain.
Other credits include Assistant Production Manager Priddy festival, Production Assistant Salisbury Festival, Health and Safety Co-coordinator Stroud Festival.

Wakas Zamurad Assistant Director

Wakas has recently graduated from the University of Huddersfield after completing his CPE. He has been a member of the Asian Theatre School for three years, before which he performed in the Sapna production of *Trust Me* (Alhambra Studio, Bradford). Whilst with the Asian Theatre School, Wakas has run workshops and has also undertaken courses in facilitating workshops. Wakas also performed in the ATS's first production *Streets of Rage* (West Yorkshire Playhouse, Leeds), and has also co-directed the recent international production of *Freeworld* (Contact Theatre, Manchester). The recent Asian Theatre School production of *Street Voices* (West Yorkshire Playhouse, Leeds and Theatre in the Mill, Bradford) saw Wakas directing a 15 minuet short as well as performing in two others. Wakas was the Assistant Director of *Silent Cry* in the regional tour of 2003, and has been brought on in the same role for its national tour.

Jeremy Nicholls Lighting & Video Designer / Visuals Director

Jeremy trained and worked at Theatre in the Mill, Bradford whilst completing his degree in Electronic Imaging and Media Communications. As a Company Stage Manager and more recently as Lighting and Video Designer he has worked with Open Hand (*Beauty and the Beast, The Snow Queen, Monster and Frog Mind the Baby*);

Twisting Yarn (*The Siege of Loving Terms, Rajpathe Badsha Lear, Legacy: An Urban Thriller, The Honoured Guest*); Frantic Assembly (*Underworld, Tiny Dynamite* – with Paines Plough & Contact, *Heavenly, Peepshow* – with the Lyric Hammersmith & Theatre Royal Plymouth); Peshkar (*The Beautiful Violin, Just Before the Rain*); Oily Cart (*Moving Pictures, Conference of the Birds*); Bigfoot Theatre Company (*Cake)*; Red Ladder (*Soulskin, Tagged).*

Ivan Stott Composer

Ivan has worked in theatre for over fifteen years; initially as an actor and for the last ten years as a composer/sound designer. He still occasionally performs as an actor/musician. Ivan's credits include numerous shows for Red Ladder Theatre Company, Sheffield Crucible, The West Yorkshire Playhouse, Theatre Centre, Half Moon, Interplay and M6 to name but a few. With Young People Ivan has facilitated work across the country and in Japan and Romania. For BBC Radio 4 Ivan composed the music for the Sony Award nominated *Blast.*

Marcus Rapley Set Builder

Marcus has been involved in theatre production for the last 20 years following a degree in civil engineering. He spent the early part of his career as Theatre Manager at Theatre in the Mill, Bradford. He now lives in Leeds and runs his own business, MJR Theatre Services and had worked with a whole range of cultural organisations including: Open Hand; RJC Dance, Sakoba Dance, Museum of Science and Industry, Manchester, Opera North, West Yorkshire Playhouse, Red Ladder Theatre Company, Leeds City Varieties. He is also currently involved in outdoor and club-night events as production manager, designer/maker, sound and lighting designer and equipment supplier.

Leslie Travers Set Designer

Leslie trained in theatre design at the Wimbledon School of Art. Designs include: *Swan Lake* – K-Ballet, Tokyo, Japan (Winner of Japan Theatre Awards, Best Production 2004); *Shirley Valentine* – Derby Playhouse, Derby; *Majnun* – 30 Bird Productions, Riverside Studios, London; *Les Contes des Hoffmann* – Folks Theatre, Stockholm, Sweden; *The Nutcracker* – E-less, Paris; *The Lark Ascending* – English National Ballet; *Taj* – The Big Picture Company, UK Tour; *Faust* – German National Films, international cinema release; *The Nutcracker* – Oxfordshire Touring Theatre Company', UK tour; *B et B*, Compagnie Pascoli, Grenoble, France; *Death by Heroin(e)* – 30 Bird Productions, Riverside Studios, London; *Vérieté* – Lindsey Kemp Company, World Tour; *Die Fledermaus* – Gulbenkian Theatre, Canterbury; *Some?* – Turin Ballet Theatre, Turin, Italy; *Vurt* – Contact Theatre, Manchester; *The Elixir of Love* – New Sussex Opera, Gardiner Centre, Brighton. He has designed a number of shows for Red Ladder Theatre Company and the Asian Theatre School, including *Tagged*, *Freeworld*, *Soulskin*, *Streets of Rage*, *Wise Guys* and *Hold Ya*. He also recently won a prize for his designs for Heinrich Marschner's *Hans Heiling* at the European Opera Awards. As well as theatre, Leslie has designed numerous pop videos and television commercials in the UK and Europe.

Seamus Finnegan Dramaturgy

Seamus is a playwright and lecturer. The author of over twenty plays, his work has been produced in the UK, USA, and Israel. His plays are studied in universities in Germany, Spain, Scandinavia, Finland and Canada. Five volumes of his plays have been published (Marion Boyars Ltd and Harwood Academic); other information can be found in the *Dictionary of Literary Biography: British and Irish Dramatists since World War Two* and the *Theatre Guide A-Z of Worlds best Playwrights*.

Sarah Brigham Co-Director

Since graduating from Bretton Hall Sarah has worked as an actor & director for such companies as BBC Radio 4 (*The Wrong Side of the River Trilogy*), The West Yorkshire Playhouse (*Summer Shorts*) and York Theatre Royal (where she is currently Youth Theatre Director). Sarah's touring credits include work with: The Theatre Company Blah,Blah,Blah, Red Ladder Theatre Company, Big Fish and Proper Job Theatre (where she was Associate Director for 2 years). Sarah has worked across Europe particularly in Berlin where she has trained community artists and directed for the Kick Company. For Asian Theatre School & Red Ladder Sarah has co-directed *Streets of Rage*(West Yorkshire Playhouse) and both tours of *Silent Cry*.

Madani Younis Writer & Co-Director

Madani Younis studied on the MPhil in Playwriting at the University of Birmingham under the tutelage of April De Angelis, David Edgar and Richard Pinner. Madani has worked nationally and internationally as an arts practitioner with both writers and actors. Appointed in 2002 as the Director of Red Ladder Theatre Companiy's Asian Theatre School Madani has successfully completed three productions for the company. *Streets of Rage* (2002), a response to the Bradford riots of 2001, achieved a sell-out run in both Bradford and Leeds. *Silent Cry* (2003). *Freeworld* (2004), an international collaboration with the Studio Theatre Damascus, Syria, which explores contemporary notions of terror and terrorism. As the Director of the Asian Theatre School Madani strives to offer and empower young British Asian actors with an opportunity to learn their craft as performers. In the spring of 2005 Madani will work closely with Red Ladder Theatre Company in scripting its devised show *Free Falling* that will go on to tour nationally. In the autumn of 2005 Madani will begin work with the Asian Theatre School on its new show that will be a collaboration with the West Yorkshire Playhouse, Leeds, that will culminate in a two week run to open the venues autumn season.

RED LADDER
THEATRE COMPANY

The Company, founded in 1968, has a colourful history that spans thirty years, from the radical socialist theatre movement in Britain known as agitprop, to the company's current position.

Red Ladder's Mission: To inspire and challenge the lives of young people.

Red Ladder works to deliver:
– A high quality theatre experience for young audiences.
– National tours
– New work
– After show work
– The Asian Theatre School (ATS)

Wise Guys by Philip Osment (2002 Tour) Sean Cernow, Daniel Abelson, David Bell & Simon Hadfield
Photo Kippa Mathews

The ATS first began as a week long summer school project in 1997. It was set up by Red Ladder Theatre Company out of the recognition that young Asian people were not accessing drama schools or theatre and that no artistic activity was available for young Asians in Yorkshire. A series of summer schools, specialist workshop weekends, and performances followed until the employment of a full time director. Over the last three years the project has gone from strength to strength culminating in the first ever national tour of the Asian Theatre School's, Silent Cry in 2004.

Red Ladder is acknowledged as one of Britain's leading national touring companies and produces high quality new plays for new and young audiences.

 Arts Council England and Leeds City Council fund Red Ladder.

 Asian Theatre School has been funded by the Regional Arts Lottery Programme and Arts Council Grants for National Touring.

Red Ladder Theatre Company
3 St Peters Buildings, York Street, Leeds LS9 8AJ
Tel: 0113 245 5311
Email: info@redladder.co.uk
www.redladder.co.uk

Directors' Notes

The privilege of listening to the stories of families who had lost relatives through a death in police custody had a huge effect on how we moved this piece through the rehearsal process and finally through to performance. The issue of course impassioned and provoked us but it was seeing the families not only having to deal with the grief of losing someone but also having to contend with such a profound injustice that really directed how you then approached the piece not only as a director but ultimately as a stakeholder in this society which has a duty to open this issue up and tell this story.

The bravery of the families and the individual's battle to find their voice and make it heard was without doubt an inspiration and a driving factor in the energy we approached the play with.

Theatre is the natural tool for telling the emotional journey such an issue forces.

The power of the emotions the characters rollercoast through are ones we all recognize but hope we never to have to contend with all at once. This play demands you to see how a family survives, implodes, then fights to survive again as they are bombarded with the debris of such a situation from all angles and how we the public watch on silently.

During both productions of the play, the dedication, commitment, humour and talent of the creative team and cast has made the process a pleasure to explore, thank you for all of it and for helping to get us all here.

Sarah Brigham & Madani Younis
August 2004

Writer's Notes

If the truth be known I was afraid to write *Silent Cry*. Having sat and cried with the families of those who had lost loved ones in Police custody, the thought of attempting to try and put pen to paper and offer a reflection of their lives scared me. The world within which they lived was a dark and cold place, the effects of a flawed judicial system could be heard in their voices, but yet in their eyes I could see a profound hope that the souls of their loved ones would not rest in peace until justice had been served. The lives of these men and women were no different to ours, except their hopes and dreams were crushed by a system that we all live within.

The experience of writing *Silent Cry* taught me that as people we can choose to accept the world for what it is, or we can strive to discover a truth that is more profound and unsettling than we could ever imagine.

The tears I shed as I sat and listened to the families of those who had lost loved ones in Police custody are memories I will carry with me for the rest of my life.

May God grant the souls of those who have died in Police custody peace.

Silent Cry is my tribute to those who continue to fight for justice.

Madani Younis
August 2004

silent cry

Autumn Tour Schedule 2004

15 & 16 September	Theatre in the Mill, Bradford
17 & 18 September	Theatre Royal, York
21 September	MAC, Birmingham
22 & 23 September	Contact Theatre, Manchester
27 September	Batley Town Hall, Batley
2 October	Rotherham Arts Centre, Rotherham
5 October	Phoenix Arts Centre, Leicester
8 & 9 October	Barbican, Plymouth
12 – 16 October	Lyric Hammersmith, London
19 & 20 October	Sherman Theatre, Cardiff
23 October	Unity Theatre, Liverpool
1 November	Oldham Coliseum, Oldham

silent cry

First published in 2004 by Oberon Books Ltd
521 Caledonian Road, London N7 9RH
Tel: 020 7607 3637 / Fax: 020 7607 3629
e-mail: oberon.books@btinternet.com
www.oberonbooks.com

A catalogue record for this book is available from the British Library.

ISBN: 1 84002 507 7

Cover image by Barry Darnell
Cover photograph by Duncan Grant

Printed in Great Britain by Antony Rowe Ltd, Chippenham

Characters

SAFIA AHMED, Mother

BASHIR AHMED, Father

ARIF AHMED, Eldest son

NADEEM AHMED, Youngest child

NOREEN AHMED, Widow

SHAHID KHAN, Arif's best friend

NINA DESAI, Civil rights activist

/: Represents the inter-cutting of dialogue

To
the memory of Kamran Khan
and to
those who are not afraid to speak out for truth and justice

Scene 1

The actors are seen on stage as the audience enter and the following scene unfolds before them.

Early evening. The Ahmed home and garden will be represented as an open plan space. NOREEN is seen hypnotically staring at a self-help book. SAFIA AHMED enters. Neither character inter-acts with each other, they merely move out of the other's way when necessary.

A projection on the back wall of a clock reaching 8.00 pm is seen. SFX of a person gasping for breath is heard. As the clock finally reaches 8.00 pm the house lights snap out and the moment is broken by the entrance through the back door of an exuberant NADEEM.

NADEEM: Mum… (*Neither responds.*)… Bhabi*… (*Neither responds. He shakes his head disappointedly cynically.*) … Sorry I didn't hear that. What was that Mum? 'How's my day been?' Yeah so so, fixed the breaks on my car in the morning, and then met some of the boys and we well… (*Checks to see if anybody is listening.*) decided we'd go and spend the afternoon in Pakistan. It was really good, thanks for asking. We ended up shopping and caught up with Chacha Shaukat. He looked different. I swear Mum he did. (*Pretends to whisper.*) He had 'love handles' that would give Humpty Dumpty a complex. Oh yeah! He sends his Salam. He said to tell you he's thinking of coming over in the summer. But enough about me. How's your day been?… (*No response.*)… Wow!! It sounds like you've been really rushed off your feet. You should get some rest, all that running around can't be good for you… I didn't see you there Bhabi. What's this? Is it new? (*He picks up the self help book.*) … *Peace and tranquillity for the soul* – 'Dr Vladimir Shmits explores ways of achieving inner peace.' That sounds…sounds… really nice. Is it helping?… (*Aside.*) I can see it's working wonders. I really enjoy our chats/

SAFIA: Does nothing useful ever come out of your mouth?

* Sister in law

17

NADEEM: What?

SAFIA: He's not in Pakistan/

NADEEM: Who?

SAFIA: Chacha Shaukat. He lives in Luton and he hasn't called your Father since/

NADEEM: I was joking.

SAFIA: I don't see anyone else laughing.

NADEEM kisses his teeth.

Silence.

NOREEN: How was it today?

NADEEM: What do you reckon?

NOREEN: Did you actually wait around to see him this time?

NADEEM: I was sat there counting the seconds go by.

NOREEN: But you *did*/

NADEEM: Yes I *did*. I don't understand what you think that sandal-wearing hippy is gonna do for me.

NOREEN: May be if you let him, he might actually help/

NADEEM: He helps give me a headache and he talks too much.

NOREEN: What does he talk about?

NADEEM: Probably the same things that are in those books of yours.

NOREEN: Did it help?

NADEEM: Do *they* help you?

NOREEN: Sometimes.

NADEEM: I think he needs to borrow some of your books then cos he's crap!

NOREEN: You didn't see him did you?

NADEEM: Just for the record you're turning into my mum. And for the second time *yes* I did see him.

NOREEN: So what then?

NADEEM: We sat. We chatted, and then he gave me a lollypop. Look, I've just wasted twenty minutes of my life listening to Gandhi and Mother Teresa's love child telling me how I should feel. I don't need you on my back as well.

NOREEN: It's been seven months/

NADEEM: What, do you think I'd forgotten?!! And by the way could you tell Mum and Dad this isn't working anymore. They won't listen to me.

NOREEN: He's only trying to help.

NADEEM: Help me do what? He doesn't even know me!!

NOREEN: None of us know who you are anymore.

NOREEN leaves NADEEM.

SAFIA: (*Opens a box of Fox's biscuits.*) Take one. The women at work sent them for you and Nadeem.

NOREEN: Tell them thank you.

SAFIA: They think I don't hear them?

NOREEN: Who?

SAFIA: The women who give me these biscuits to bring home for you every day. I know who they're talking about when I walk into the canteen, but I don't say anything. And then they smile and wave at me and tell me to come and sit with them. They even offer me some of their pink wafers to have with my cha.

NOREEN: I love those pink wafers.

SAFIA: (*Reluctantly.*) Exactly.

NOREEN: They must really like you then?

SAFIA: The company gives us pink wafers as a treat. But *they* all give their pink wafers to me because they feel sorry for us.

NOREEN: Don't worry, they'll find something else to talk about soon enough.

SAFIA: It doesn't matter anymore. What's happened, has happened. It's Allah's will to decide/

NADEEM: Mum… Mum!!

SAFIA: I might be old, but I am not deaf. Ha?

NADEEM: Aren't you supposed to be at that meeting with Dad?

SAFIA: I had to work a few extra hours/

NADEEM: But you got in before me?

SAFIA: Since when did you become my Father?

NOREEN: Did you call and tell Dad?

SAFIA: Don't worry, it's too late anyway. The meeting's probably already started. His phone will be switched off.

NADEEM: But Dad said he wanted you to be there/

SAFIA: These meetings aren't helping to pay the bills. Someone in this house has to remember to work/

NADEEM: But I thought Dad said/.

NOREEN: Nadeem! Just listen to your Mum.

NADEEM: Listen to Mum?! She just wants to forget it ever happened. You know she wasn't/

NOREEN: Nadeem that's enough we've heard you already/

SAFIA: Oh suddenly he's not afraid to tell everyone how he feels.

NADEEM: See I told you/

SAFIA: They all know our business. What more do they want to hear?

NOREEN: You don't mean that do you?

SAFIA: Look they won't listen to us. We can't change the past. It's kismet.*

NADEEM: Kismet?!!

SAFIA: Why don't you do something other than screaming at us?! Go to that meeting and tell the whole world how wrong they are and how right you are? You're just like him. Selfish/ (*NADEEM stares angrily at his Mother and rushes into the garden where he proceeds to light up a cigarette.*) I know what it is you do out there. You can tell your precious Father what it is when he gets back from his meeting. (*Pause. Trying to hold back the tears.*) When did my own child forget who brought him into this world.

NOREEN: He hasn't forgotten.

Lights change.

Scene 2

NINA DESAI of the Fight for Justice campaign is giving a passionate address at the local community centre. BASHIR and SHAHID are sat listening attentively on either side of her.

NINA: … I spend my days listening to the stories of families who have lost loved ones and I ask myself how many more times will one of us have to die before something changes. Arif Ahmed was someone's son, someone's husband, someone's brother.

The Fight for Justice organisation will not give up the fight. We will not stop shouting. The truth will out. Justice will be served. Arif Ahmed did not die in vain. His death at the hands of the Police was no accident.

* Fate

Why can't we see or hear what they did to Arif in that custody suite? What are the Police doing to help Arif's family? Will his death be just another sad forgotten statistic?

We can change the future. We can change the future today if only we find the strength to unite as a community and support the family at a time when they need us the most.

SFX Applause is heard as NINA takes her seat.

BASHIR: (*Leans over to NINA.*) Nina your words mean a lot to us all. (*Pause.*) I don't know what happened to Safia tonight. She said she was feeling a bit ill this morning. That's probably what it is, and I haven't checked my phone all day, she probably left a message/

NINA: It's OK you don't have to explain, it happens to a lot of families. Not everyone feels comfortable coming to meetings like this.

BASHIR: I must go see Haji Rehman before he leaves.

BASHIR exits.

NINA: Shahid how's Nadeem been with you?

SHAHID: Still finding it hard. You know I was watching everyone listening to you when you were talking. You make a difference to all of them and obviously to us as well.

NINA: I'm glad you think so.

SHAHID: I don't think anyone can just stand up and say the things that you just did.

NINA: You could probably do it if you wanted to?

SHAHID: (*Sarcastically.*) I don't think so.

NINA: You knew him better than anyone else.

SHAHID: I aint no speaker Nina.

NINA: You should think about it.

SHAHID looks away awkwardly.

You sell cars you shouldn't be afraid of talking to new people.

SHAHID: It's not really my kind of thing.

NINA: I think Arif would have appreciated it.

SHAHID: I don't think so! C'mon be serious, I'm not really speaker material now am I?

NINA: You don't look too bad.

SHAHID: Whatever.

NINA: No really I think you look good.

SHAHID: (*Smiles.*) Yeah?

NINA: But your hair?

SHAHID: What's wrong with it?

NINA: It's, it's… (*Searching for words.*) Well it's different.

SHAHID: 'Different'? (*Mimes licking both his hands, and then proceeds to create a geeky-looking centre parting in his hair.*) How about now?

NINA: (*Giggles.*) We need to work on it.

SHAHID: You think?

NINA: Don't worry, we'll get there.

SHAHID: I won't hold my breath.

NINA: Under the circumstances that's probably a good idea. (*Pause.*) I'm always around if you need any coaching.

SHAHID: Yeah?

NINA: Of course. I think you've got a lot of talent.

SHAHID: You're probably the only one that does.

NINA: Just give me a call when you get some time. We'll work on it.

SHAHID: Yeah I'll give you a call.

Lights change.

SFX breathing and clocks ticking.

Scene 3

Family home.

SAFIA: Why don't you tell your Father what it was you were doing outside?

NADEEM: Dad, Mum said she missed you.

BASHIR: Tell your Mother that there will be another meeting tomorrow, and if she's not too busy, it would be good to see her there.

NADEEM: Mum, Dad's gonna be late in tomorrow, he's out on the pull.

BASHIR: Oi batameez*! Is that what I told you to say!!

NADEEM: He's working late.

SAFIA: Tell him his food will be in the oven.

NADEEM: Mum said you'll have to cook for yourself.

BASHIR: What is wrong with you tonight?

NADEEM: Well if you heard what Mum said, why do you keep asking me?

SAFIA: Tell your Father he'll have to check the boiler, the water isn't getting hot.

NADEEM: Dad the boiler's on the blink again, it needs fixing.

* Someone without manners

BASHIR: Ask your Mother why she tells me this five minutes after I've just got in?

NADEEM: You ask? (*BASHIR stares sternly at him.*) … No you're right, what was I thinking, I'll ask. Mum, Dad said he'll take a look at it tomorrow.

SAFIA: OK. Is that tomorrow as in tomorrow, or tomorrow as in next week when the kitchen ceiling decides it wants to get to know the kitchen floor a bit better?

NADEEM: I'll just check that for you. I think Mum wants it doing now Dad.

BASHIR: I'll have to ask Rashid to check it tomorrow when he finishes work/

SAFIA: Tell him not to ask that good for nothing Rashid to check it. It's because of him it's like this now.

BASHIR: You know what the problem with Mir-Puri women is son?

NADEEM: You're gonna tell me anyway aren't you Dad?

BASHIR: Nothing can wait till tomorrow.

NADEEM: Mum, Dad says he loves you.

SAFIA: Nadeem have I told you about Mir-Puri women?

NADEEM: I can't wait for this.

SAFIA: If Mir-Puri women waited for everything to happen *tomorrow*, I'd still be waiting to give birth to you and your brother.

NADEEM: Just for once can you two just get along. (*Exit NADEEM.*)

NOREEN: How was it?

BASHIR: Busy. Nearly eighty of them that came to support the campaign, even Haji Rehman was there with his sons.

SHAHID: Salam Auntie.

SAFIA: Walikum Salam Shahid. It was good?

SHAHID: Nina spoke well. She impressed a lot of people.

BASHIR: Bethi*, even some Mothers came from the community to support the campaign. Imagine that, Mothers who have not even lost their own children came to support our Arif's campaign.

NOREEN: It's good that people are finally listening to what happened.

SHAHID: Someone from the paper was there.

NOREEN: Did you speak to them Dad?

BASHIR: No I left it to Nina. She has a better way with words.

NOREEN: I hope they write something good about him this time.

BASHIR: She seems to think they will.

NOREEN: It might stop everyone talking/

SAFIA: Shahid was Samina there? Samina who runs the clothes shop near the sports centre?

SHAHID: Yeah I think/

SAFIA: Well maybe you should think about who you let into your meetings Shahid.

BASHIR: Noreen, it's good that people still remember your husband?

NOREEN: Yeah of/

SAFIA: How long did it take for her to start gossiping with the other women?

SHAHID: I don't/

---

* Daughter

BASHIR: Maybe it would be good for you to come to the next meeting.

NOREEN: I'll think/

SAFIA: Did Nina speak about Arif ?

SHAHID: Not just Nina/

BASHIR: You know people are actually starting to give money to the campaign?

NOREEN: That'll help make a/

SAFIA: How many of her own children does she have?

SHAHID: I don't think she has any.

Awkward silence.

NOREEN: Why don't you get some rest, you've been at work all day?

SAFIA: You're right it's a shame no one else seems to like working anymore.

NOREEN: I'll get you your tablets.

SAFIA: I haven't gone mad yet, I know where they are kept. Only Allah knows why I still have all my senses about me living under this roof. (*Exit SAFIA looking tired and frustrated.*)

SHAHID: Where's Nadeem got to?

NOREEN: He's outside. He had a bit of a rough day with the counsellor.

SHAHID: He went back again? But I thought after the last time/

NOREEN: Yeah, Dad said he should try again. I think he'd be happy to see you.

Lights change.

Scene 4

Garden.

NADEEM: You just get here?

SHAHID: Yep.

NADEEM: They told you/

SHAHID: Why do you think I'm stood in the mud?

NADEEM: Right.

SHAHID: Good day?

NADEEM: Same old. And you?

SHAHID: Busy.

NADEEM: Sell that Golf?

SHAHID: Ah ha. Meeting went off well. (*Pause.*) You know that will kill you? (*Cigarette.*)

NADEEM: I've got an idea. How about you go fuck yourself?

SHAHID: I'll pretend I didn't hear that.

NADEEM: You weren't there. You don't know what it's like living with that lot.

SHAHID: How many times have we had this conversation? It's not easy for them/

NADEEM: Save your breath. I know how this one goes.

SHAHID: (*Awkward silence.*) What was he like?

NADEEM: He made Mary Poppins look like Hannibal Lecter.

SHAHID: Sounds like you had fun, you stay long?

NADEEM: Twenty minutes.

SHAHID: Twenty minutes. Twenty fuckin' minutes Nadeem?!!

NADEEM: I timed it on my watch. Well to be exact it was twenty minutes and ten seconds.

SHAHID: Shit!

NADEEM: I know.

SHAHID: (*Shakes his hand.*) Well done! I know that must have been hard. That might even be a bit of a record for you. And there's your sister in law telling me it went badly. I should shake his hand, it's a fuckin' miracle that you managed to stay still for twenty minutes and ten seconds.

(*Both men laugh.*)

NADEEM: I thought I'd try and make an effort for my Mum and Dad. I don't think it really worked.

SHAHID: Look. Leave it with me I'll sort it. I tried you on your phone earlier.

NADEEM: I was at the garage. You can never get reception in there.

SHAHID: What were you doing?

NADEEM: Trying to fix the break pads on my car/

SHAHID: How'd you get on?

NADEEM: What do you think?

SHAHID: Bring it round and I'll have a look at it tomorrow.

NADEEM: Cheers. (*Pause.*) You reckon we'll bother opening the garage again?

SHAHID: I don't know, we'll just have to wait and see. Look let's get inside before I sink into this fuckin' mud.

Scene 5

Family home.

BASHIR: We saw the solicitors again.

NOREEN: Any good news?

BASHIR: They said the transcript from the CCTV cameras are not ready yet. *Nina* said we should be patient.

NOREEN: What did the *Solicitor* say about it?

BASHIR: He said the papers will be ready for the Inquest.

NOREEN: What about the money they found in the car?

BASHIR: He's not sure/

Enter SHAHID and NADEEM.

NOREEN: So it's true then, he really did do what they said?

BASHIR: They haven't found any new evidence.

SHAHID: Maybe something new will come out once we get the transcript back.

NADEEM: The money wasn't his, we all know that.

NOREEN: Right, of course it wasn't. I'll see if Mum's alright. (*Exit NOREEN.*)

SHAHID: Uncle it's getting late I'll leave you to it.

NADEEM: You off already?

SHAHID: Some of us have to get up early in the morning... (*Takes the envelope and gives it to BASHIR.*) Uncle take this before I forget. It's not much, but it might do something.

BASHIR: You don't have to keep doing this.

SHAHID: It's the least I can do.

BASHIR: Inshallah we'll get there eventually.

NADEEM: I'll see him out.

Lights change.

Scene 6

NINA is seen waiting for SHAHID. They share a moment of intense intimacy together.

NINA: Don't worry I won't tell your Auntie.

Scene 7

Garden. A few days later.

BASHIR is seen stood in the garden smoking. SAFIA walks past him with a washing basket under her arms. BASHIR is seen flicking his ash into the flower beds.

SAFIA: What have the plants done to you?

BASHIR: I thought you wanted me to smoke in the garden.

SAFIA: I don't mind you choosing to kill yourself just leave the plants alone.

BASHIR: I thought this was our garden.

SAFIA: When was the last time you spent any time in it?

BASHIR: If you hadn't noticed we have other things to be worrying about.

SAFIA: Why do you do that?

BASHIR: Makes me feel better.

SAFIA: That makes you feel better. What kind of example are you setting for Nadeem?

BASHIR: He's not stupid, he knows better than to start smoking. (*Pause.*) It's hard/

SAFIA: No one's forcing you to put it in your mouth.

BASHIR: Not the cigarette.

SAFIA: Oh.

BASHIR: Me having to do it all by myself.

31

SAFIA: Well Nina seems to be giving you a lot of support.

BASHIR: It would make a difference if everyone in this house gave their support. Noreen should come, it would be good for her.

SAFIA: She spends her days reading them books, she isn't ready to go. Like everyone else in this house she doesn't understand what he was doing with all that money in his car.

BASHIR: Keep your voice down, the whole street can hear you.

SAFIA: They all know our business anyway what difference does it make now. The newspapers say he was selling dangerous cars, even her (*Signalling at the neighbour's house.*) next door is telling everyone it was drugs money.

BASHIR: When did you start listening to what she had to say? We might never find out who the money really belonged to.

SAFIA: (*Holds back the tears.*) Look at us, we hardly have enough money to pay for the solicitors, and do you think any of *them* really care about what happens to us when they go their beds at night? (*Pause.*) There must be another way. Does it all have to be done through the newspapers?

BASHIR: We can only do what we think is right.

Silence.

SAFIA: You remember when your Father gave us the money to come over to this country?

BASHIR: You said you didn't want to live the rest of your life in the rain.

SAFIA: You told me your brother was already here, living like a king.

BASHIR: It wasn't a very big house was it?

SAFIA: It wasn't a house, it was a damp room, without any heating.

BASHIR: You said you liked it.

SAFIA: We'd only been married three months! Do you remember the names of all the people that shared with us?

BASHIR: I've tried for the last twenty-six years to forget about little Zulfqar.

SAFIA: I wonder whatever happened to him.

BASHIR: Let's hope he didn't become a barber. (*SAFIA laughs.*) You remember what he did to my hair?

SAFIA: It looked better after he'd finished with it.

BASHIR: There was nothing wrong with it until he got his hands on it.

SAFIA: You looked like the fourth member of the Bee Gees.

BASHIR: By the time he had finished I could have been the fifth member of the Beatles.

SAFIA: I'm sure Nadeem's got some gel upstairs, it's never too late to try.

BASHIR: I think I'm too old for that now. (*They share a moment together.*)

SAFIA: We should have stayed in Pakistan.

BASHIR: No one could've seen what would happen.

SAFIA: What did we do wrong? (*Pause.*) I dreamt it again/

BASHIR: Please Safia not now.

SAFIA: It's important that you know/

BASHIR: I've heard this before/

SAFIA: Did your Mother never tell you about her dreams?

BASHIR: They never came true/

SAFIA: Of course they did, you should have listened to her.
I dreamt that there was a snake in our house.

BASHIR: What?

SAFIA: It went through all the rooms and not even you
could stop it.

BASHIR: I'm tired of all your stories.

SAFIA: Please just listen/

BASHIR: We have a strong case. This will all be over soon.

SAFIA: Why don't you ever listen to me?

Silence.

BASHIR: Look we'll find the answers we want. Nina said
it's a strong case.

SAFIA: 'Nina said.' How can this women talk so much
about my son? She never met him. She didn't change his
nappies when he was a baby, or held him when he was
sick with the flu/

BASHIR: Nina has dealt with cases like this before, she
knows what she's doing.

SAFIA: But what does she want from us?

BASHIR: Why don't you ask her yourself? She'll be here in
a few hours. (*He puts out his cigarette, and returns back to
the house.*)

SAFIA is left alone, hanging the clothes in the garden.

Lights change.

Scene 8

Garage. NADEEM is seen smoking.

NADEEM: They use to be lined up all the way from in here
down to the bottom of the street.

SHAHID: It's a shame that none of them wanted to pay him properly, he might have got somewhere bigger than this.

NADEEM: He said it was good PR to work on his friends' cars. He reckoned they would tell other people how good a mechanic he was.

SHAHID: You remember that Merc he kitted up for 'Little Nav'?

NADEEM: Oh yeah, it looked like shit!

SHAHID: It's a shame your brother didn't tell him. It might have stopped him driving around the area carrying on like a pimp.

SHAHID / NADEEM: Dickhead!

SHAHID: He still lives at home you know.

NADEEM: With all that money he's spent on that car he could've brought his Mum a house in a nice white area of town.

SHAHID: What's his Mum gonna do in a nice white area of town?

NADEEM: That's true. But I bet he gets some girls?

SHAHID: I could tell you some stories about me and your brother before he got married, and stopped coming out with the boys.

NADEEM: He told me everything already.

SHAHID: Everything?

NADEEM: Yeah, even about the time that girl's brother came looking for you/

SHAHID: He didn't tell me she was a Patan.

Silence.

NADEEM: One day I want all of this/

SHAHID: All of what?

NADEEM: I want to run this garage like Arif did.

SHAHID: You told your parents about this career move?

NADEEM: They won't understand/

SHAHID: I wonder why.

NADEEM: Do you reckon I can do it?

SHAHID: You can barely fuckin' change break pads. I don't think you're quite ready for all of this yet.

NADEEM: Why not? It was good enough for him. It's an honourable job.

SHAHID: You go to college, and you want to be a fuckin mechanic, do you know the kinds of crooks and liars that work in this game?

NADEEM: But you sell cars. You and Arif were even in business together.

SHAHID: You think I sell cars out of choice?

NADEEM: Fuck off Shahid I can make up my own mind.

SHAHID: (*Pause.*) Look, you're too much of a pretty boy to be getting your hands all covered up in grease.

NADEEM: Maybe I don't want to be a grease monkey. Maybe I'll start selling cars and go into competition against you.

SHAHID: (*Looks at his watch.*) Oh shit!! I told your Dad I'd have you back in time for when Nina got there. C'mon let's lock this place up.

NADEEM: Shahid?

SHAHID: What?

NADEEM: About the garage. It was just a thought/

SHAHID: What have I told you about thinking?

Lights change.

Scene 9

Family home.

Kitchen.

SAFIA: (*Looks at BASHIR and NINA sat on the couch.*) Does she have no respect for herself?

NOREEN: What?

SAFIA: How can she sit so close to him?

NOREEN: Dad doesn't seem to mind. (*Smiles cheekily to herself.*)

SAFIA: What does he know anyway? His precious little Nina is perfect/

NOREEN: She probably doesn't know it's wrong.

SAFIA: She seems to know everything else.

NOREEN: You should tell Dad that you don't like it.

SAFIA: Ha!! As if he listens to me anymore.

Front room.

BASHIR: Do you enjoy this?

NINA: What do you mean?

BASHIR: All this kind of work that you do?

NINA: I think so.

BASHIR: You never really hear about women doing *this* kind of work do you?

NINA: I think that's slowly changing now.

BASHIR: I've never heard of a Ms Gandhi, or Ms Luther King?

NINA: I don't think you've looked hard enough.

BASHIR: Maybe some day they'll have a special day to remember you by.

NINA: We'll just have to wait and see.

BASHIR: I'm sure they won't forget you.

NINA laughs politely.

BASHIR: Where I grew up you never saw a woman talking the way you do in public

NINA: You think it's wrong?

BASHIR: Oh, no, no. Not wrong just different. I think it's very good what you do.

NINA: (*Confused.*) Thanks.

BASHIR: It's different for our people.

NINA: Not anymore.

BASHIR: His Mother's afraid to do what you do.

NINA: People deal with it differently.

BASHIR: It's a shame there are not more women like you.

Enter SHAHID and NADEEM.

SHAHID: Auntie it was my fault, I lost track of time.

SAFIA: She's here already.

SHAHID: How long has she been waiting?

NOREEN: Not long.

BASHIR: Where have you been? (*Directed at NADEEM.*)

SHAHID: It was my fault Uncle. Sorry Nina.

NINA: That's OK, I was just catching up with Bashir. (*Enter SAFIA and NOREEN.*) Hello Safia, how have you been?

SAFIA: Very well thank you, and you?

NINA: Fine, how's work?

SAFIA: The same. Someone has to remember to pay the bills.

NINA: That's good. And you Noreen, how have things been? Bashir tells me you've been reading a lot of books lately, anything interesting?

NOREEN: I'm finding them quite/

SHAHID: Has the Solicitor been in touch?

NINA: That's why I'm here.

NADEEM: You got the transcripts from the CCTV.

NINA: Yeah.

NADEEM: Have you read it?

NINA: I have. (*Pause.*) It's very graphic. (*Takes the transcripts out of her bag and hands them to the family.*) It's all there in black and white. (*As each member of the family are given the document they begin to read it.*)

SFX The following distorted voices are heard as a voice over whilst the family read the transcript. Disjointed images are seen.

A bell sounds. And a door is heard shutting.

PC 1: And who's this?

PC 2: A Mr Arif Ahmed.

PC 1: And to what do we owe the pleasure.

Sounds of heavy breathing are heard.

PC 1: What's he doing that for?

PC 2: He's been trying on that dying swan routine all the way in. He's just pretending.

PC 1: Pick him up off the floor and take them cuffs off.

PC 2: He fancied himself a bit, he was fronting on us when we arrested him, he tried it on with PC 2754 on the way in. It took both of us to restrain him.

PC 1: What's that smell? Has he vomited?

Breathing gets louder.

PC 2: PC 2754 said he was threatening, and he got aggressive so I got my gas out. I didn't actually squirt him, but I know I'll have to put a use of force report in.

PC 1: What did you pick him up on?

PC 2: Speeding.

PC 1: What's he doing in here then?!

PC 2: He started acting suspiciously when we pulled him over. Found fifteen grand in his glove box. Wouldn't tell us how he came to have it.

PC 1: You seen him before?

PC 2: Nah. His licence says he's from/

PC 1: C'mon let's hurry this along. It's still early and there's plenty more of his sort to come in yet.

Breathing stops.

PC 2: He's not making any more of them noises.

PC 1: There's fucking blood coming out of his mouth. How long has he been bleeding?

PC 2: I don't know.

Breathing continues.

PC 1: Where's PC 2754? He's not fucking breathing lads!

PC 2: Shall we call an ambulance?

PC 1: You better get an ambulance now…dead quick

PC 2: 18 (call sign).

PC 1: Put him on his side.

PC 2: 18 (call sign). Yeah can we get an ambulance to control, to CCO over.

PC 1: Thump his chest... Put him in the recovery position! Put him in the recovery position!!... Get his head back.

NADEEM drops the transcript and runs out of the room.

PC 2: Have we got an airway...which way up do these bloody things go?

PC 1: No not like that, yeah like that, that onto his face that onto you.

PC 2: Feel for his pulse...

PC 1: C'mon Arif don't fuckin' die on us!!

PC 2: That's the ambulance, c'mon let's get them doors open for the paramedics.

Voice-over fades out.

The family sit in silence for a moment. Noreen and Safia are seen crying.

BASHIR: Will they listen to us now?

NINA: This will make a difference but there's a long way to go before/

NOREEN: (*Clearly upset.*) What more do they want to hear?! He died at the hands of the Police and you're not sure. What is there left not to be sure of?

BASHIR: We should just listen to Nina/

SAFIA: Listen to who?/

SHAHID: Auntie c'mon it's hard for everyone. Noreen we'll find out who it was that killed Arif I promise. We just need to be patient for a little bit longer.

SAFIA: Has this not gone on long enough, when will it all stop?

NINA: The Police Complaints Authorities have never found one of their own men guilty of a death in custody.

BASHIR: But we've got evidence now.

NINA: I know. We'll just wait and see what happens.

Tense silence.

SHAHID: What's next?

NINA: The transcript and CCTV footage will be used at the Inquest hearing in three months. It will be up to the jury to decide/

NOREEN: But what about the money? (*The transcript.*) Do they know where he got all that money from?

NINA: I know it's hard for you. But no new evidence has come about. I think we have to accept Arif was involved in some kind of making and selling of illegal cars/

SAFIA: Illegal cars?

SHAHID: She means ringers.

SAFIA: What does that mean?

NINA: It's welding two different cars together.

SAFIA: Why would he do that?

SHAHID: This isn't getting us anywhere.

NINA: (*Hesitantly.*) I think what will help to make a difference to Arif's case is if you thought of joining a wider campaign with other families who have also lost loved ones in custody.

BASHIR: But you just said this would make a good difference.

NOREEN: Isn't it too early to start joining other campaigns? We're so close to the hearing?

NINA: I said you should *think* about it.

BASHIR: But the case has got so much publicity over the last few months, are you sure?

NINA: By becoming part of another campaign I can tie Arif's case into the work I'm doing with the other families.

BASHIR: Can we not join another campaign later?

NINA: As important and as significant as your case is, I do work with other families. By joining a bigger campaign I can evenly spread my time between you all.

BASHIR: It sounds as if you've made the decision for us.

NINA: Bashir I don't want you to worry/

BASHIR: So what shall I do then?

NOREEN: When do we have to tell you?

NINA: I know tonight was probably not the best time to ask this of you all, but I'm not going anywhere, it's just a thought, I think you should give some time too. It's been a long day, I should go. (*NINA gets up to leave.*)

SHAHID: I'll see Nina out.

Following conversation is had as NINA is leaving the door.

NINA: I thought you said you would talk to Bashir about joining another campaign.

SHAHID: I got caught up with Nadeem.

NINA: You should have told me sooner.

SHAHID: When would you have suggested, before or after we read that transcript?

NINA: Look I want to help them, but they have to see where I'm coming from.

SHAHID: They're just scared.

NINA: Didn't you listen to a word of what I said to you the other night?

SHAHID: Look now's not a good time/

NINA: For who?

SHAHID: I have to get back inside.

NINA: Run along back to your 'Auntie' like a good little boy.

SHAHID: I'll see you later, we'll talk about it then?

NINA: I don't know why I expected you to understand.

SHAHID: I said I'll be round in a bit.

NINA: Save yourself the hassle. I'll be fine on my own.

NINA exits and SHAHID returns back to the front room.

NADEEM is stood in garden. He is seen holding a necklace.

NADEEM: What the fuck did they do to you Arif?

Front room.

NOREEN: What will happen now?

BASHIR: (*No response.*)

SHAHID: I'll check on Nadeem. (*Exit SHAHID through the back door.*)

SAFIA: Noreen give him some space, we'll work it out.

NOREEN exits. BASHIR and SAFIA are left sat some distance apart.

SAFIA: Maybe she's right?

BASHIR: When have you ever thought that she was right?

SAFIA: The campaign is not over.

BASHIR: We've only come this far because Nina's done so much/

SAFIA: But you and Shahid have helped as well.

BASHIR: Maybe she thinks we don't appreciate her enough.

SAFIA: Ha!!!

BASHIR: I've spent all my life working in the council helping everybody else.

SAFIA: We all know how hard you've worked.

BASHIR: Just look around you, what good has it done. They don't even know who I am anymore.

Lights change.

Scene 10

Later that evening. NOREEN is sat listening to a self help book. An American voice is heard on the tape. With her eyes firmly shut NOREEN carefully follows the tape's instructions.

TAPE: Now let's begin with our second step to reaching inner piece. Sit in a relaxed position, looking straight ahead of you. And then thinking of your inner being, turn your head slowly over your right shoulder and then breathe out. Feel that negative energy pouring out of your body. Breathe in as you bring your head back slowly to face the front and visualise positive thoughts. You will slowly find yourself entering a happy safe place/ (*NOREEN opens her eyes and wipes away the tears.*)

NADEEM bursts in.

NADEEM: What you doin'?

NOREEN: (*Wiping away her tears, she switches off the tape.*) Haven't you heard of knocking?

NADEEM: What's he banging on about?

NOREEN: I'm trying to relax.

NADEEM: Well?

NOREEN: What?

NADEEM: Is it working then? (*No response.*) What happened to the book?

NOREEN: I thought I'd give this a go.

NADEEM: (*Sarcastically.*) You should listen to some whale music, I heard it really relaxes you.

NOREEN: Thanks, I'll remember that.

NADEEM: (*Brings out Post-it notes from his pockets.*) So these must be yours then?

NOREEN: Where'd you get them from?

NADEEM: Found them stuck on the inside of the kitchen cupboards. I thought it was Mum that had gone mad.

NOREEN: No one's gone 'mad'.

NADEEM: So what's all this mean then. (*Starts quoting from the Post-it notes.*) 'Remember you are surrounded by beauty' – Do you think I'm ugly? And this one, 'feel the fear and do it anyway' – what's all that about? I think I feel fragile.

NOREEN: (*Frustrated.*) You wouldn't… We all need something to help us along. What have you got?

NADEEM: Whatever!

NOREEN: He said we'd have our own place in a year or so. That's why he was working so hard.

NADEEM: I knew you didn't like living here.

NOREEN: No I like it. I just wanted us to have our own place.

NADEEM: Tell the truth, it's cos you've never got on with Mum.

NOREEN: I should have told him to slow down.

NADEEM: What difference would it have made?

NOREEN: It might never have had to happen.

NADEEM: It wasn't you that killed him.

NOREEN: But all that money they found in his car.

NADEEM: It was probably the Police that put it in there.

NOREEN: Why?

NADEEM: Cos they wanted to hide what they did to him.

NOREEN: The garage wasn't making that much money, but say if it was/

NADEEM: What you talking about? He wouldn't do that.

NOREEN: May be it was, and he did/

NADEEM: Do you know why?

NOREEN: What?

NADEEM: Why he had all that money on him?

NOREEN: (*Pause.*) No.

Silence.

NADEEM: You should stop listening to this crap, it's not helping you.

Lights change.

Scene 11

Family home.

SAFIA: (*To BASHIR.*) Everything will be OK? It will all turn out alright won't it? (*BASHIR fails to respond, he gets up and exits.*) (*Pause.*) No one listens to me anymore Arif. (*Pause.*) I don't know what's wrong with all the men in this family, they're all afraid to say how they feel about anything. They just carry their anger around with them. You were everything he wanted to be. Everyone knew you, and people would stop him in the street and ask how you were. Nothing made him happier. (*Pause.*) They only stop him now to ask if you really had all that money in your car. What were you doing Arif? What kind of trouble were you in?

NOREEN: Mum what's wrong?

SAFIA: Why did this happen to us?

NOREEN: It will be OK.

SAFIA: How? It's too late now.

NOREEN: I can't imagine how much pain you're feeling right now. But you still have us.

SAFIA: What can I do?

NOREEN: This family doesn't work without you.

Lights change.

A long period of time is shown to elapse. The actions of the family show how slowly their lives are moving, and how their relationships are changing.

Scene 12

Garage.

NADEEM is seen holding Arif's necklace

SHAHID: I thought you'd be in here… (*NADEEM does not respond.*) He use to wear that when he played cricket. He said it brought him luck. He was the only person in the team that didn't need it. The rest of them could have done with a little of what he had.

NADEEM: Did you see the four of them in there?

SHAHID: Yeah.

NADEEM: Stood there like it was no big deal.

SHAHID: I saw the way you looked at them. For a minute I thought you were gonna do something stupid.

NADEEM: Do you think the thought didn't cross my mind?

SHAHID: So what stopped you?

NADEEM: We've waited three months to see them, and I almost felt excited that I was gonna finally be in the same room as them. I wanted them to see me. I wanted them to know I was his brother. I wanted to look into their fuckin' eyes and try and work out what it must be like to be a murderer.

SHAHID: Don't worry, in a few days that jury will find them guilty.

NADEEM: Look at this (*Showing the newspaper.*) They called him a 'dodgy mechanic', they even said he had been previously charged with assault. It's funny how they forgot to mention it was minor assault against some drunk that came at him after a football match.

SHAHID: Forget about it.

NADEEM: They *forget* to tell their readers how he choked to death on his own blood in a Police custody suite, and you're telling me to forget about it. If he was a dog that got run over on the street they would have given him more sympathy.

SHAHID: Look/

NADEEM: You saw it too didn't you? I could hear them saying 'Fuck off back home and stop being such a fuckin' nuisance'. They didn't want us in there telling them they'd done something wrong. They thought they were doing us a favour by just listening to us. The bastards.

SHAHID: Look why don't you stop this? You're in here, while your family are sat at home worrying themselves about where you are.

NADEEM: Doesn't this (*Showing him the newspaper.*) bother you anymore?

SHAHID: Do you know what, you're right. Some of that stuff is just lies, but not all of it.

NADEEM: What you talking about?

SHAHID: Stop kidding yourself Nadeem!! Your brother
was no angel/

NADEEM: He was no different to you?

SHAHID: Exactly.

NADEEM: He didn't keep any secrets from me.

SHAHID: You think he really told you everything?

NADEEM: Are you deaf! I just said he did.

SHAHID: He tell you about that time we stole that car
from outside the sports centre and how we drove it
around town/

NADEEM: What?

SHAHID: But someone must have rung the Police, and
before we knew it they were all over us. Stupid me drove
it into the back of a parked van, we had to run and hide
in the park all night till they'd given up looking for us.
Oh I forgot he must have told you all about that story
already?

NADEEM: He probably just forgot/

SHAHID: You don't get it do you. He was protecting you.
He wanted you to be different, but you can't see that can
you?

NADEEM: I'll be who ever I want to be!!

SHAHID: Do what you want, I don't care anymore.

NADEEM: Fuck you!! You're the same as them? (*NADEEM
rushes out leaving his brother's necklace behind.*)

SHAHID: Nadeem come back I shouldn't have said that.
Shit!! (*Picks up the necklace.*) Look at the fuckin' mess that
you've left me in.

Lights change.

Scene 13

Family home.

BASHIR and SAFIA have returned home after the Inquest hearing.

BASHIR: Did you see how many journalists were there?

SAFIA: Them journalists are only after their headlines.

BASHIR: I wonder what they will write about us tomorrow.

SAFIA: Probably the same things that they have always written about us. They stand there for hours in the rain hoping we might say something controversial, or Arif's friends might get so angry that they will start to riot in front of them.

BASHIR: You're right, they've grown tired of hearing us shout and scream.

SAFIA: No they'll keep writing they just won't put photographs of us on the front page anymore. I don't think our faces really help to sell their newspapers.

BASHIR: We'll just have to wait for the verdict on Friday.

SAFIA: I'm used to the way journalists look at us now. They are what they are. But we don't need anyone's sympathy anymore.

BASHIR: What do you know?

Silence.

SAFIA: I dreamt I saw him again/

BASHIR: Not now. Please it's been a long day.

SAFIA: No it was good. I saw him. He was dressed up all smartly. He smiled at me, he said, 'It will all be OK'.

BASHIR: Ever since we buried him in Pakistan you have been having these dreams. None of them have helped us.

SAFIA: This one was good/

BASHIR: It was good for you! Did your dreams tell you why Nina wasn't at the hearing today?

SAFIA: Things will be better. Arif said 'It will all be OK.'

Enter NOREEN through the back door.

NOREEN: Salam.

Awkward silence.

SAFIA: How's your Mother and Father?

NOREEN: They're doing well.

SAFIA: Did you tell them what happened today?

NOREEN: She's praying it will all turn out alright for us. (*To BASHIR.*) It was a shame Nina couldn't be there today, I'm sure she will come tomorrow. We're slowly getting there aren't we?

BASHIR: Let's just be patient until Friday. (*Exit BASHIR.*)

SAFIA: I know I haven't been much help to you, but what's happened to you in the last few months, where have you found this strength from?

NOREEN: I've gone back to more traditional methods.

SAFIA: He would've been proud to see the way you are coping with it all now. You shouldn't be shy to ask your parents to come and eat with us. This is your home as well.

NOREEN: It doesn't feel the same without Arif.

SAFIA: Don't be silly, you will always have a place here. Nadeem would be lost without you.

NOREEN: He's learning to cope better/

On cue NADEEM charges in, and frantically looks behind him. He pauses for a moment, and begins to empty his pockets out onto the table.

SAFIA: What's happened?

NOREEN: What's wrong? What have you lost Nadeem?

NADEEM: You wouldn't understand/

SAFIA: (*Puts her hands on either of his arms.*) Sit down. Nadeem sit down! And tell me what's happened?

NADEEM: Mum it's better you don't know/

SAFIA: Just tell me/

NADEEM: I did something stupid/

SAFIA: Its alright just tell me what's happened.

NADEEM: It's all his fault/

NOREEN: You're not making sense. Whose fault?

NADEEM: Who do you think?

NOREEN: Nadeem!!!

NADEEM: Your husband's/

NOREEN: Stop being so stupid and tell me what you did.

NADEEM: (*Begins to cry. He fights back the tears.*) Did he tell you everything? Did Arif tell you everything he ever did?

NOREEN: What's this got to do with anything?

NADEEM: Answer the question. Did he tell you everything!

NOREEN: Yes he told me everything. Now tell me what happened to you?

NADEEM: If he could tell you everything. Why did he have to lie to *me* then?

NOREEN: About what?

NADEEM: I don't need to tell you, you know everything there is to know about him already.

SAFIA: Calm down. You're scaring us. What did you do?

NADEEM: (*Breathse deeply. Brings out a big permanent marker from his jacket pocket.*)

SAFIA: What is this for?

NADEEM: I wrote all over the back of a Police van.

NOREEN: Why would you do something so stupid?

NADEEM: Use your imagination. But then/

SAFIA comforts NADEEM who begins to cry.

SAFIA: What did you do then?

NADEEM: I didn't check… There were Police officers sat in the front of the van/

NOREEN: Oh that's really clever/

SAFIA: Don't you think that we haven't got enough/

There are two loud knocks on the back door.

NOREEN: Did they see you?

NADEEM: Maybe they/

Another knock.

NOREEN: Don't move.

NOREEN opens the door, and SHAHID enters. Everyone breaths a sigh of relief. NADEEM sees SHAHID and pushes his Mother away.

SHAHID: What's happened?

NOREEN: Ask Rolf Harris over there.

SHAHID: You alright?

NADEEM: Yeah.

SAFIA: Talk some sense into him. (*To NOREEN.*) Come let's leave them to it.

NADEEM continues to look through his pockets.

SHAHID: (*He brings out the necklace.*) Is this what you're looking for? You left it at the garage. (*Pause.*) So what is it? What did you do now?

NADEEM: What do you care anyway?

SHAHID: He only ever had one brother, no one can ever take that away from you/

NADEEM: Is that all you came to say?

SHAHID: I actually came over to say sorry. But do you know what forget it, here have it. (*Gives NADEEM the necklace.*) You can't keep living like this. You can't change the past, none of us can.

SHAHID exits, NADEEM is sat on his own. He holds back the tears and walks outside into the garden to have a cigarette. BASHIR, unaware of what has happened, walks into the garden and lights up a cigarette. They share a moment as they realise what the other is doing. It is a somewhat bizarre Father and Son moment. They continue to smoke.

BASHIR: Busy night.

NADEEM: Yeah.

BASHIR: (*Notices the necklace.*) He use to wear that when he/

NADEEM: Played cricket I know.

BASHIR: I gave that to him on his first match. I told him I wore it when I scored my first century/

NADEEM: I didn't know you played?

BASHIR: Oh no I never played cricket, I left that to your uncles/

NADEEM: But you told him/

BASHIR: He was feeling nervous. I thought it would help him play better.

NADEEM: Yeah it did the trick.

Lights change.

Scene 14

Garage.

NINA: Sorry. I forgot where it was. So this is where it all happened then?

SHAHID: They missed you at the hearing today.

NINA: (*Sarcastically.*) No I'm fine thanks. I can't hold everyone's hand.

SHAHID: That's not fair. You should have called, Bashir was worried.

NINA: I didn't mean that sorry! Look I've been at meetings all day trying to raise money for Arif's campaign and everyone else's for that matter.

Silence.

SHAHID: I've left messages on your phone all week.

NINA: I've been busy.

Pause.

Look. Maybe it's not such a good thing/

SHAHID: Us?

NINA: There was no 'us'. It was just 'A', 'A'/

SHAHID: You should have said if you didn't like it.

Awkward silence.

I guessed that's why you wanted to see me.

NINA: I should have been more professional.

SHAHID: What?

NINA: I said professional. If the press got wind of it, imagine what they would do to me/

SHAHID: So what?

NINA: You don't understand/

SHAHID: Since when have the press cared about you?

NINA: Lets just forget this/

SHAHID: No c'mon Nina I thought it was about the families/

NINA: What you saying?

SHAHID: When did you forget this is all about Arif Ahmed and not about fuckin' Nina Desai.

NINA: I've been doing this well before Arif died, and I'll be doing this long after his case has reached a conclusion.

SHAHID: What do you get from all of this?

NINA: A sense that I'm changing something/

SHAHID: No you don't. You *want* your face in the paper.

NINA: Shut up!

SHAHID: So it's not working out the way that you wanted it to. What you gonna tell Bashir and/

NINA: I've tried to help Arif's family but your 'Auntie' doesn't want me in the house, and the family aren't comfortable with all the press attention. I think it's better if I give them some space to cope with this as a family. You and me hasn't helped the situation.

SHAHID: Or may be you just need to move on to someone else/

NINA: It's just not the/

SHAHID: Don't bother, what's there to tell anyway?

NINA: I'll try and see Bashir and the family tomorrow.

SHAHID: You feeling guilty?

NINA: Do you? (*NINA exits.*)

Lights change.

Scene 15

SAFIA is heard finishing off a conversation with the next door neighbour.

SAFIA: … We'll hear the result on Friday. You shouldn't believe everything you read. If a Mother can't fight for her children what can she fight for? Inshallah* the Police men that did that to him will be punished. Please pass that onto the other sisters for me…

NOREEN is in the kitchen. NADEEM is sat holding Arif's necklace in his hands.

NOREEN: Oi! Has Mum given you back your colouring pens yet?

NADEEM: What's happened to you?

NOREEN: When?

NADEEM: What's been making you so happy over the last few weeks , someone told you the verdict already?

NOREEN: No.

NADEEM: All them self-help books must really work then?

NOREEN: The only thing they helped to do is make someone else richer.

NADEEM: So what is it then? You been seeing your Mum a lot lately, she asked you to go back and live with them? Wouldn't blame you if you did. I'd do the same thing, any excuse to get out of this madhouse.

NOREEN: Yeah you're right, it was my Mum/

NADEEM: So when you off?

NOREEN: I'm not off anywhere. I prayed with her/

NADEEM: You did what?

* God willing

58

NOREEN: Prayed/

NADEEM: For who?

NOREEN: For us/

NADEEM: (*Unimpressed.*) Oh right, that was good of you.

NOREEN: When we were little kids she would always send us to Mosque to pray and read the Quran after school.

NADEEM: (*Cynically.*) Wicked/

NOREEN: I didn't get why she did it. I just wanted to watch cartoons like my other friends did.

NADEEM: (*Sarcastically.*) I've got Scooby-Doo on video upstairs if you want to watch it/

NOREEN: You don't get it do you?

NADEEM: Get what?

NOREEN: It gives me strength/

NADEEM: Praying?!

NOREEN: You shouldn't dismiss it until you've tried it.

NADEEM: So has *he* told you why it happened then?

NOREEN: It's not about that, no one can change what Arif went through/

NADEEM: Just by praying you've got a new found strength? Don't make me laugh.

NOREEN: What do you suggest, I just mope around the house like you do, and bite off anyone's head that says something I don't like?

NADEEM: Praying isn't gonna bring him back, going to them meetings isn't making any difference/

NOREEN: What should we do Nadeem?

NADEEM: You can't have known him that well if you're finding it so easy to move on!

NOREEN: (*Takes off her ring and throws it at him.*) Take it. Pick it up!! Pick it up!!! There you have it, since you're the only one that cares about him so much you should have it! Do you think any of us will ever forget? Do you think I don't think about him every minute of the day wishing he was here with me now, so I didn't have to listen to you crying like a baby? It's not just you that hurts/

Enter SAFIA to see the two of them stood opposite each other almost suspended in time.

SAFIA: What is this? Nadeem?… (*No response.*) Noreen?… (*No response.*)

A knock at the front door is heard.

NADEEM: I'll get it.

NADEEM and NOREEN exit in opposite directions. SAFIA is stood alone. NADEEM returns with NINA DESAI.

Take a seat I'll just go get him for you. (*Shouts at the top of his voice.*) Dad!! Dad Nina's here!

BASHIR enters the front room and takes a seat.

NINA: I should have called to tell you I was coming over. I've been so busy I just didn't have the time/

BASHIR: We missed you at the Inquest.

NINA: Sorry/

BASHIR: Has something happened?

SAFIA: Let Nina speak.

NINA: (*Nervously.*) I've been busy fundraising. A lot of people donated generously to the campaign.

BASHIR: This means we can tell more people about what happened to Arif?

NINA: I hope so/

NADEEM: You hope so?

BASHIR: Nadeem!! So what do we do now?

NINA: I've decided. I mean Fight for Justice has decided to use the money to bring on a new junior assistant. I'm hoping they will spend time working on your case/

BASHIR: What does this mean?

NINA: I don't want you to worry. I'm going to still work on Arif's case. But our new assistant will do most of the work surrounding his campaign.

NADEEM: So you're leaving us then?

NINA: Like I said I'll still be around, but I need to spend time working on some of the other cases that I have outstanding at the moment.

SAFIA: Who is the new person?

NINA: We haven't appointed them yet. Look, we're not abandoning your family, we just need to facilitate the case in a more productive manner.

NADEEM: What you saying now?

NINA: You have my number, and I'll be at the Inquest on Friday to hear the verdict with you all.

NADEEM: Dad?

NINA: It will be fine Bashir.

BASHIR sits motionless.

I'll leave you all to think about it (*NINA exits.*)

SAFIA: It's not the end of the world. We'll get through this, she said someone else will help. We brought Arif into this world, he was our son, we can do/

BASHIR: Do what? When did you care about the campaign? We've only got this far because of her. Who's going to listen to us now?

SAFIA and NADEEM leave the room. BASHIR stares aimlessly.

Lights change.

Scene 16

Garage.

SHAHID: What do you think that jury will say tomorrow?

NADEEM: Whatever they want.

SHAHID: You made it up with her yet?

NADEEM: What for? She hates me.

SHAHID: So you gonna spend the rest of your life in here avoiding her?

NADEEM: Probably.

SHAHID: When is this all gonna stop?

NADEEM: What?

SHAHID: You.

NADEEM: I didn't ask you to be here.

SHAHID: You make me laugh.

NADEEM: I'm glad someone still finds me funny.

SHAHID: Open your eyes, your family loves you, and you're carrying on like a fuckin' dickhead!

NADEEM: You've told me this before.

SHAHID: Then do something about it? (*Pause.*) Arif made mistakes like everyone else. Just cos he didn't share them with you, doesn't mean he didn't care/

NADEEM: He didn't have to protect me.

SHAHID: Imagine if he did tell you, what would you have done? Gone home and told your Mum?!!

NADEEM: Why don't you stop following me around like my shadow and fuck off!!

SHAHID: I'm glad he didn't tell you everything/

NADEEM: Go on then, tell me what he did? I want to hear all about it. It doesn't matter now anyway does it?

SHAHID: Leave it/

NADEEM: No I want to hear all about my big brother?

SHAHID: Fuck off!

NADEEM: Tell me!! What you scared of?!!

SHAHID: (*Grabs NADEEM by the neck and pushes him against the wall.*) Do you want to hear that your precious brother made ringers in this garage. And you know what? He was actually quite good at it as well? That's the only way he could make any money out of this place. I don't know if you've noticed but the streets around here aren't exactly paved with gold.

NADEEM: So you did it, you sold that car to that bloke in Manchester? But you told the Police you didn't know how he got all that money?

SHAHID: He would have done the same thing/

NADEEM: (*Pushes SHAHID away from him.*) You bastard it should have been you in the car not him. He wasn't meant to die/

SHAHID: He didn't die cos he sold a fuckin' ringer, the Police killed him, you've even seen them at the hearing.

NADEEM: It's blood money. All of it, everything you've given to the campaign – it's from selling them cars?

SHAHID: It's the same money he would have given to you on a Friday night when you went out with your friends.

NADEEM: You fucking/

SHAHID: So you gonna tell everyone the big secret then? What difference will it make, its not gonna bring him back /

NADEEM: Yeah you're right I'm gonna tell everyone. I'm gonna tell the whole fuckin world that his best friend stitched him up. That it should have been you, and not him. *You* don't give a fuck about anybody except yourself. (*NADEEM picks up a wrench.*)

SHAHID: Put that down before you hurt yourself/

NADEEM: Its not me I'm gonna hurt. (*NADEEM goes at SHAHID with the wrench.*)

SHAHID: What you doing?!!!

NADEEM is seen beating the shit out of SHAHID with a wrench.

Lights change.

Time is shown to elapse. Things feel like they are taking forever to reach their end.

Scene 17

Family home.

A month has passed. NOREEN is in her room praying, she is sat on the floor on a prayer mat. During this scene the images of the last few minutes of Arif's life are projected onto the back wall. She slowly begins to put on the traditional head scarf.

NOREEN: … Allah it's been hard for us all. But you've looked over us through out these hard months. Allah, I thank you for giving me the strength to cope. I thank you for the family you have given me, and for the few months that I had with Arif. Allah, tell him I loved him for who he was. Tell him he brought happiness into all of our lives and that we forgive him for what he did. He wanted the best for his family. Allah, tell him how much I miss having him around me.

Allah, look over his family when I leave. Grant your blessings to his parents, allow them to find the strength to come together and be happy once more. Look after Nadeem, he has a good heart he's just confused. Ameen.

Scene 18

Garden.

SAFIA: How have you been? (*No response.*) It looks like Noreen picked up some more leaflets from the printers. (*No response.*) Can you believe the women's group at the community centre have asked me to talk about Arif's campaign? I didn't think anyone cared any more/

BASHIR: You've worried more about your precious garden than you have about your own son's campaign.

SAFIA: Forget about the garden, the flowers will grow back again next year. It's been a month. So the verdict didn't go our way, it doesn't mean it's the end/

BASHIR: They said his death was a lawful killing. They think the Police were right to do what they did. The case is finished with now.

SAFIA: They have never found a Policeman guilty before, why would they make an exception for us?

BASHIR: This is all just a test/

SAFIA: But it's not over, we can fight on.

BASHIR: All this because you had a dream. (*Silence.*) May be we should just move on, Arif will never come back to us now. Let us just carry on with our lives/

SAFIA: You work in the council, you know how long it can take to make a difference.

BASHIR: We might both be in our graves before a difference has been made to his case.

SAFIA: But let's try while we still can? I don't want to die thinking I didn't fight. Arif wouldn't want us to stop.

BASHIR: It's just us now. Nina nor her assistant call anymore, they've all given up. Even his best friend doesn't come to the house anymore.

SAFIA: Shahid will come back, he's just been busy. The others didn't know Arif like we did. He will always be a part of our lives. We don't need to wait for Nina.

BASHIR: I'm tired.

Scene 19

Garage. NADEEM is seen by himself holding his brother's necklace in his hand.

NADEEM: I didn't think I had it in me. You should have told me he was a dickhead! He kept going on about how you would've done the same thing. But he got what he deserved. It felt good to wipe that smile off his face the lying bastard. (*Pause.*) I hope he don't come round and tell Mum and Dad, they'd hit the ceiling. I'm trying to make things better between us. It's taking a bit longer than I thought.

I'm sorry about what I said to Noreen. If you were here I know you'd probably have given me a slap. I wouldn't blame you either. I'm surprised she didn't do it herself. I promise I'll sort it out with her it's about time I did something useful.

You know what people like us don't belong here, but fuck it I ain't going anywhere.

He hangs his head in frustration.

Scene 20

Family home.

NOREEN: Is Dad OK?

SAFIA: He just needs time. It's been hard for him, he'll soon come round.

NOREEN: I don't know what to say to make it better?(*Pause.*) I want to tell you something/

SAFIA: Have the solicitors called?

NOREEN: No, not today.

SAFIA: Is it Nadeem?

NOREEN: You worry too much. You know I'm grateful for everything you all have done for me/

SAFIA: You have done more for us/

NOREEN: I don't know how you've put up with me at times/

SAFIA: It's not been easy for any of us. You are a part of this family too/

NOREEN: I will always see you as my family/

SAFIA: What's happened?

NOREEN: I want to go back and live in my parents home. I mean I'll be back, I'm not running away from you all or anything. I think it would be good just for a while to go back.

SAFIA: Who could blame you if you did/

NOREEN: I think it will be good for me. You know I'll never/

SAFIA: It's alright, I think you should.

NOREEN: You do?

SAFIA: We all need to carry on. He wouldn't have wanted us all just to stop. We'll keep fighting. Are your parents happy/

NADEEM enters.

NADEEM: Salam Mum. You alright Bhabi?

SAFIA: Did you go and speak to your tutor?

NADEEM: I'll do it tomorrow?

SAFIA: You said that yesterday?

NADEEM: Mum I'll do it, I've just been busy today.

SAFIA: We'll talk about this later. I have to get ready/

NADEEM: You off out/

SAFIA: Speaking at the community centre. (*Exit SAFIA.*)

NADEEM: I didn't think she would ever do it by herself.

NOREEN: We all change don't we?

NADEEM: Why you looking at me like that?

NOREEN: You haven't called me 'Bhabi' in months.

NADEEM: So what's new?

NOREEN: (*Pause.*) I'm moving back home.

NADEEM: It's cos of me isn't it?

NOREEN: It's not you. I just think it's the right time/

NADEEM: I can tell you're still angry with me, cos of that time I said them things?

NOREEN: You'll still see me most days I don't live that far away/

NADEEM: (*Unwraps a tissue from his pocket, and gives NOREEN her ring back.*) Here he gave it to you, anyway it doesn't suit me?

NOREEN: It will be OK. Let's check on your Dad.

As they walk into the front room, we hear the intro to the local news. Leading the news is the voice-over of NINA DESAI who has taken up another high-profile case of a young man who has died on this occasion in Police custody. BASHIR switches the television off.

NINA: (*Voice-over.*) I spend my days listening to the stories of families who have lost loved ones and I ask myself how many more times will one of us have to die before something changes. Richard Stevens was someone's son, someone's husband, someone's brother.

Underlying this moment is the sound of someone gasping for breath. The projection shows the point of view of someone washing their hands. This point of view will pan up and look straight into a mirror. In the reflection we will see the reflection of a panicked Policeman looking back at us. The image will look at us for a few moments before it dissolves to black.

Lights change.

Scene 21

SAFIA is seen addressing the women's group at the community centre. She speaks in both Urdu, and English.

SAFIA: Our children are our children. We bring them into this world. We watch them fall. We hold them when they cry. We tend to them when they are ill. We pray to Allah to protect them from pain and suffering. As Mothers we all know there is nothing harder than watching your child suffer in front of you. If you could you would take that pain away from them in a heartbeat. Sometimes they forget to say thank you. Sometimes they might think they know more than us. But still they are our children.

You have probably heard the name Arif Ahmed already. Arif Ahmed was my eldest son. He died at the hands of the Police, and I couldn't help him when he needed me the most. He might have done some things that were wrong, but I will always love him, he was mine, I brought him into this world.

We all know what it is to have children, but few of us know what it is like to see them die. I ask you all to help support me and my family. Now all we have is memories. Others shouldn't have to go through this.

Lights change.

The End.